HOPE
FOR THE BEST
PLAN
FOR THE REST

WORKBOOK

APPLYING THE 7 KEYS FOR NAVIGATING A LIFE-CHANGING DIAGNOSIS

DR. SAMMY WINEMAKER
DR. HSIEN SEOW

Copyright © 2025 by Dr. Sammy Winemaker and Dr. Hsien Seow

All rights reserved. No part of this book may be reproduced, stored in a retrieval system or transmitted, in any form or by any means, without the prior written consent of the publisher, except in the case of brief quotations, embodied in reviews and articles.

This book is not intended as a substitute for the medical advice of physicians. The reader should regularly consult a physician in matters relating to their health and particularly with respect to any symptoms that may require diagnosis or medical attention.

Cataloguing in publication information is available from Library and Archives Canada.

ISBN 978-1-77458-557-3 (paperback)

Page Two
pagetwo.com
Edited by Kendra Ward
Copyedited by Steph VanderMeulen
Cover and interior design by Jennifer Lum
waitingroomrevolution.com

*To everyone bravely working to put the human back at the center of care.
Collectively, we can and will create change.*

CONTENTS

Introduction *1*

1. **From "In the Dark" to "In the Know"** *5*
2. **Walk Two Roads** *11*
3. **Zoom Out** *21*
4. **Know Your Style** *35*
5. **Customize Your Order** *47*
6. **Anticipate Ripple Effects** *59*
7. **Connect the Dots** *71*
8. **Invite Yourself** *81*
9. **Putting It All Together** *91*

Conclusion *97*

Acknowledgments *99*

INTRODUCTION

Dear Reader,

You may not realize it yet, but in your hands you have something powerful that is going to change your illness experience. This workbook will help you to articulate who you are as an individual, express what is important to you, and identify the most relevant questions to ask—all of which will ensure you have an illness journey that best represents *you*! Readers of our book, *Hope for the Best, Plan for the Rest: 7 Keys for Navigating a Life-Changing Diagnosis*, on which this workbook is based, have told us that the information within increased their hope, choice, and control. Some have described the book as "empowering" and wish they had read it earlier.

For decades, Sammy, a palliative care doctor who works in people's homes, has cared for thousands of patients and their families during the late stages of the patients' illnesses. Hsien, a palliative care researcher, has interviewed thousands of patients, their families, and health care providers to understand how to improve care. It has been clear to us for a long time that many patients and families are suffering. Too many feel overwhelmed, unprepared, frustrated, and scared. Along the illness journey, patients and families feel reduced to a diagnosis, an organ, or even a number.

Several years ago, we started working toward a simple goal: to improve the illness experience for people facing a life-changing illness. We began to reflect on the stories of the thousands of patients and families we had cared for and interviewed. We uncovered seven keys that unlocked a better illness experience. These seven keys are powerful because they are actions that can be initiated by patients and their families at any point in the illness journey. The keys are a way to lessen the power gap that exists between patients and the health care system. They help patients and their families reclaim some control and choice.

Over the past few years, we have shared the seven keys with the public in many ways—through a website, a podcast, social media, speaking engagements around the world, and most importantly, our book, *Hope for the Best, Plan for the Rest*. It was designed as an essential guide for every patient and their family, with practical steps showing them how to be an activated patient or caregiver.

The response, especially to the book, has been overwhelmingly positive. We have received so many messages about how the seven keys have been a game changer for patients and their families. The keys have given patients a new language with which to talk with their health care providers. Families are suddenly "unfrozen" and start to move forward with decisions. Most importantly, the book has given patients and families renewed hope while they deal with uncertainty and plan for the future.

Hope for the Best, Plan for the Rest has been adopted by patients, families, and health care providers all over the world. They have recommended the book to others, hosted book clubs, taught webinars, donated books to libraries and doctors' offices, adapted the content for pamphlets and posters, and even created buttons.

In fact, people keep asking us for more—mainly for a workbook and a course. So, we listened.

How to Use the Workbook

The goal of this workbook is to enable you to have an illness journey that puts *your* needs, not the health care system's needs, at the center. Although you may not be able to control your illness, you can control many aspects of your illness experience. The chapters here follow the order of the seven keys in our previous book. While we recommend reading the book first, you can use this workbook on its own. You can follow the chapters in order, though you don't have to, as the keys are not sequential. You might also find it helpful to go through the workbook over time rather than try to complete it all at once.

In each chapter, we start with a brief summary of the key, followed by a reflection. Next, we provide exercises, some of which are also accessible through QR codes throughout this book. Finally, we answer commonly asked questions by patients and families. As you work through each key, you may want to skip certain exercises if they aren't relevant to you or you don't feel ready to do them yet.

The exercises will teach you how to extract essential information you may not have known was available. You can take control and have more human-centered care by role-modeling and inviting your health care providers to see you as an individual who is seeking open and truthful information. Many health care providers are waiting for this invitation. It is a chance to let down their guard and an opportunity to tap into the beauty of relational care and authentic connection, which is why many chose a health care profession in the first place.

At the end of the workbook is a one-page summary called "My Big Picture." It pulls from a few important exercises in the chapters to create a personalized snapshot of you told through the seven keys. It is meant to be at the heart of your care journey and to guide you, your family, and your health care providers.

Who Can Benefit from Reading This?

Although this workbook is written for patients, it can and should be used by those close to you as well. Throughout this workbook, we use the terms "family" and "inner crew" synonymously to describe your chosen family, which may or may not be blood-related. These people may be your spouse or life partner, your children or parents, close friends and neighbors, or others.

We encourage you and your family to complete the exercises individually and discuss them together. In the FAQs, we also directly address some common challenges brought forward by families and caregivers. As well, exercises in this workbook should be shared with your health care provider and can act as a bridge across common communication barriers.

Health care providers will benefit from reading this workbook, particularly those who are frustrated because care has become transactional rather than relational. Providers can use activities in this workbook to put the human back at the center of care by inviting patients and their families to engage in more open discussions about what to expect over the course of the patient's illness.

Finally, the workbook can be useful even if you aren't currently facing a life-changing illness. We've met many people who just want to be better prepared or better able to support others on their illness journey.

Are You Ready?

During a life-changing illness, you may sometimes feel hopeless. But this workbook is full of hope. This workbook will help you identify, seek, and acquire information you need. The exercises will equip you with the skills to ensure that you remain *you* along the way.

We're excited for you to learn how to take control and feel empowered!

Grab a pen, and let's get started.

Sincerely,

Dr. Sammy Hsien

Dr. Sammy and Dr. Hsien

1

FROM "IN THE DARK" TO "IN THE KNOW"

Our years of experience have revealed that patients and families facing a life-changing illness can generally be divided into two categories: those who have an "in the dark" illness experience, and those who are "in the know." When you are in the dark, you feel overwhelmed, scared, and unprepared. When you are in the know, you feel more confident and prepared and that you have more choice and control. This chapter helps you identify whether you are having an in the dark illness experience, and if so, how to become more in the know.

Reflection

Like so many people we've met, you may have fears about being sick. They may stem from your prior experiences observing or caring for someone in your past. Or perhaps you have been sick before. Your exposure to illness throughout your life will influence how you receive a new diagnosis. Things you see on TV, in movies, and on other media may also influence your thinking, sometimes adding a dramatic twist to your imagination and creating unrealistic fears.

People feel many emotions along the course of their illness. They may feel scared, angry, worried, and anxious at times. These feelings are all valid. When ignored, sometimes they bring about unhelpful coping mechanisms like avoidance, procrastination, or escapism, which can be barriers to being in the know. You may be surprised to learn that fears can be eased with information. Information is the antidote to feeling in the dark.

Prompt: What different emotions have you felt along your illness journey so far? What are you most worried about?

EXERCISE 1.1: In the Dark or In the Know?

Rationale: This exercise can help you get a sense of whether you are more in the dark or more in the know at this point.

Instructions: To measure how you feel on your illness journey so far, circle where you rank on the scale.

In the dark					In the know
Reactive	1	2	3	4	Prepared
Unaware	1	2	3	4	Informed
Unsure	1	2	3	4	Confident
Depersonalized	1	2	3	4	Individualized
Overwhelmed	1	2	3	4	In control
Frustrated	1	2	3	4	In charge
Scared	1	2	3	4	Hopeful

Do you rank more toward the in the dark or in the know side? If you are more in the dark, don't worry. This workbook will help you shift to an in the know experience. If you are already in the know, this book will help you stay there.

EXERCISE 1.2: Define a Life-Changing Illness

Rationale: This activity is designed to help you better understand the nature of your illness. We have met many people who don't know if they have a life-changing illness and what that means exactly, which prevents them from being prepared.

Instructions: Circle yes or no in response to the statements below. If you aren't sure of the answer, ask your health care professional.

My illness is chronic, meaning it cannot be "cured," it cannot go away, and I will have to manage it for the rest of my life.	Yes No
My illness is progressive, meaning it is likely to get worse over time.	Yes No
My illness is life-limiting, meaning that having the illness will likely shorten my life expectancy compared to if I didn't have it.	Yes No

If you circled yes for *any* of the above questions, you have what we would consider a life-changing illness. As such, throughout your illness, you will face many decisions that affect you, your life, and those you love. Therefore, you'll want to gather information and be in the know as early in the illness as possible so you can make the best decisions for yourself.

EXERCISE 1.3: How Ready Are You to Be In the Know?

Rationale: The key to being in the know is being as informed as possible. Having a broad understanding of your illness is powerful. But how ready are you for the full picture? The following quiz will help you assess.

Instructions: On a scale of 1 (not at all) to 5 (extremely), circle the option that best reflects you for the following questions:

How important is it for you to have information about the reality of your illness?

(not at all)   1   2   3   4   5   (extremely)

How ready are you to learn more about your illness?

(not at all)   1   2   3   4   5   (extremely)

How much is it in your nature to seek information?

(not at all)   1   2   3   4   5   (extremely)

Scoring: Add up your score. If your score is 9 or more, then you're on your way to being in the know. If your score is 8 or less, then you are at greater risk of being in the dark. Don't worry if you scored 8 or less. For many people, their natural tendency is not to seek information. And they don't know what they don't know. But this workbook can help.

An in the know experience hinges on your willingness to be informed about the reality of your illness, for better or worse. If you feel hesitant to seek information because you worry about what you'll hear or find, that is to be expected. Patients begin their journeys at different stages of readiness. Nonetheless, our experience is that those who have more information have a better, more grounded illness experience. Information will help you adjust and move forward.

We encourage you to go through the exercises in the rest of the book at your own pace, so that you are equipped to get more information. You can be scared and fearful while also being brave and curious to find out what you need to know to be in the know.

2

WALK TWO ROADS

TO WALK TWO ROADS means to hope for the best and plan for the rest. It is the most important key and often the hardest to achieve. Everyone wants to be positive around someone facing a life-changing illness. We want people to be hopeful. And hope must be aligned with where you are at in an illness. This chapter invites you to seek realistic information and consider what-ifs while you stay positive. You will use this skill often, especially when the illness changes or you face a decision. Planning ahead will protect you from feeling reactive and crisis-driven.

Reflection

People have different degrees to which they can be hopeful and realistic at the same time. However, in our experience, patients are often waiting for permission to get real about their illness. People will tend to be constantly positive around you. When positivity becomes toxic, though, you may feel pressure to be upbeat all the time, too, which may feel silencing.

Prompt: Do you feel pressure to be constantly positive? Is there anything you wish you could talk about?

EXERCISE 2.1: Declare Your Preference

Rationale: If you want to explore the road of "planning for the rest," this exercise will help you share your preferences. One way to invite your inner crew and health care providers to walk two roads alongside you is to role model walking two roads and declare your intention for this balance.

Instructions: Below are statements about being hopeful and realistic. They invite those around you to consider open communication about the reality of your illness. Circle which statement feels most like you:

a   I'm grateful for your positivity. However, to support me best, I want you to know that we can walk two roads, which means being hopeful while also being realistic about what is happening in my illness.

b   Thank you for your support and positivity. Let's also be as realistic as possible together. If it's okay with you, let's try to balance hope with open communication about what's going on as things change.

c   Thank you for being my cheerleader. I also give you permission to speak to the difficult and scary things we are facing, too. I don't want to shy away from the hard stuff.

If none of these fit, try writing your own:

_____

_____

_____

_____

_____

_____

_____

_____

EXERCISE 2.2: Start Walking Two Roads

Rationale: Being able to hope for the best and plan for the rest will keep you feeling grounded and in control. But often, it's hard to know how to start. If you aren't sure how to begin, try out this exercise.

Instructions: First, identify things you are hoping for at present. Second, consider things you are worried about or what you might need to plan for based on your understanding of your illness. Go as far into the future as you would like, and stop at a point when it feels uncomfortable. Just looking ahead is a step forward.

Example

At this stage of your illness journey, what are you hoping for?

1. I am hoping my treatment works.
2. I am hoping I can stay and be cared for in my own home.
3. I am hoping I have enough energy to attend my child's wedding at the end of the year.

Which what-if scenarios are you worried about or might you prepare for should things not go exactly as planned?

1. What if this treatment stops working?
2. What if I can no longer care for myself at home?
3. What happens if I cannot drive anymore?

Now you try.

At this stage of your illness journey, what are you hoping for?

1 _____
_____
_____
_____

2 _____

3 _____

Which what-if scenarios are you worried about or might you prepare for should things not go exactly as planned?

1 _____

2 _____

3 _____

EXERCISE 2.3: Let Your Mind Wander

Rationale: If you completed the previous exercise, congratulations! You have started to walk two roads. You were able to list your hopes and also think about what-ifs and things you are worried about.

Instructions: Look at your list of what-ifs. Give yourself permission to let your mind wander. Consider what plans you could start exploring sooner rather than later.

Examples

What if: my treatment stops working?
I could: create a list of questions for my doctor, make a list of people in my life who will be able to support me, and explore what services are available to me.

What if: I can no longer care for myself at home?
I could: understand options for community in-home services, tour other possible settings of care, discuss the option of moving in with a family member or vice versa, and explore paid help.

Now you try.

What if: _____

I could: _____

What if: _____

I could: _____

What if: _____

_____

I could: _____

_____

Tip: Share the information from exercises 2.2 and 2.3 with your inner crew and your health care providers so you can talk openly about how realistic your hopes are and how best to achieve them. Discuss whether the what-if scenarios are realistically matched to where you are in your illness, and what supports and resources are available if those what-ifs happen. And don't forget to repeat these two exercises as new information or concerns arise, treatments change, or decisions need to be made. Together, what-ifs and I coulds are at the center of hoping for the best and planning for the rest.

EXERCISE 2.4: Help Health Care Providers Face "the Other Road"

Rationale: Health care providers want to be helpful, but you may find that your quests for more information about what-ifs are ineffective, for a variety of reasons. We created this activity to help you respond to a reluctant health care provider.

Instructions: Your health care provider may avoid your questions in a variety of ways. Below we list some of the most common scenarios and what you might say in response.

They seem too busy and appointments are too short.	"You are so busy. I don't want to disrupt the flow. When is a good time for me to ask you some questions?" "Could we make a specific appointment to discuss my burning questions, perhaps one that is a bit longer or at the end of the day?" "Is there someone else on the team who would be better to ask these questions of?"
They don't seem to know what to say.	"I know this is a big question. You have my permission to speak openly."
They seem uncomfortable with emotion.	"Please don't sugarcoat things because you worry about my reaction. I'd prefer information straight up."
They seem concerned that talking about the future will upset you.	"Even if you trigger my feelings when we discuss the reality of my illness, I will adjust and use the information to move forward."
They seem to have their own agenda, and it's hard to speak up.	"I appreciate that you have things to cover in this appointment. Heads up: I'll need a few minutes to ask some questions."
They seem to be avoiding questions concerning more information about the future.	"Understanding the reality of my illness is important to me and will make me feel a better sense of control."

FAQs: Walk Two Roads

I just got a new, scary diagnosis and no one wants to talk about it. How do I start to walk two roads?

The first step is to gather information about your illness. Do an Internet search of reputable disease or health care organizations. Read books about your illness and pamphlets from your doctor's office. Talk to other people who have a similar illness, or join a local disease-specific support group. Once you have the information, invite other people to hear what you've learned. Explain how the information helps you feel more empowered and realistically hopeful. Declare that you can hope for the best while planning for the rest! (Try exercise 2.1.)

What if the illness is diagnosed at a very late stage? Planning for the rest feels like planning for the end. How can we walk two roads when time is short?

No matter how short time might be, you can still have hope—for comfort, for life closure, for the enjoyment of relationships, and so on. A short illness course is often shocking. But any chance to quickly gain facts about the situation will likely result in some degree of adjustment to it, and allows hope to be realistic.

Help! My loved one doesn't want to know. They don't want to talk about the future at all. I think they are in denial. How can I help them walk two roads?

Denial is when a person declares something true to be untrue—like a patient saying, "I'm not sick." We call this "big D" Denial. It is quite uncommon. However, sometimes people avoid entertaining the truth about their situation because it is too upsetting. They may not want to talk about it openly or they may insist on trying different treatments even when they have been told they won't work. We call this "little d" denial. It is a common coping mechanism that kicks in when a person is not ready to face an uncomfortable situation. Everyone moves through an illness differently and at their own speed. It is okay. The good news is that most people's minds will eventually align with their bodies so that they can see what's in front of them. Gently invite them to walk two roads with you, but don't push too hard.

How do I handle different approaches to talking openly about the future in my family? I want to walk two roads, but a family member is trying to "protect" our loved one from the truth. What can I do?

When people exhibit varying degrees of readiness to speak openly, it often reflects how things were prior to the illness. If you think a family member is protecting a loved one from knowing facts about their illness, you might start by trying to understand how tender topics are typically discussed in the family. This might reveal cultural or religious reasons or just how your family deals with challenges. It is worth asking the person with the illness what they want shared within the family. You can also ask loved ones what they understand and what information they would like to know. Sometimes, families are surprised that the loved one knows much more than they realized.

When someone is sharing—with strong emotions, language, or reactions—about how hard they find it to face their illness, what can I say or do instead of being falsely positive?

Just listen. The person obviously feels comfortable enough to share this with you. You don't have to shut them down. Let them get it off their chest. Reflecting back their experience and identifying the emotions may help. You might say something like, "I really appreciate how open and honest you are with me about your feelings." Feelings are normal, and often, people feel better when they are given an avenue to share raw emotion. You don't have to fix the emotion. Your presence is often the best medicine.

FOR MY BIG PICTURE

Which of the following statements best represents you? Circle all that apply.
a It is important for me to have hope.
b I want to get realistic information about my illness.
c I would like people to communicate with me openly.
d I am not ready for more information yet.
e Other: _____
_____

3

ZOOM OUT

EVERY ILLNESS HAS a well-established pattern and general trajectory over time. The key Zoom Out shows you the road map of your illness so you understand where you are now and what to expect in the future. This information is grounding and helps you feel more in control. All too often, people get lost in the day-to-day business of their illness and lose sight of the big picture. You might zoom out often, especially when your illness changes or you have a decision to make.

Reflection

Sometimes, having the big picture of a situation helps you make decisions, plan, and/or move ahead with confidence. For example, when planning your career, you need to map out the education and training requirements to reach your goals. Without a plan, you might feel lost or unsure of what to do next.

Zooming out to see the big picture of your illness gives you important context about where you are and where you may be heading. If you need to make a decision during a crisis, you may feel rushed and unsure, especially if you have not planned for it.

Prompt: Think of a time when you were going somewhere new and got lost. There was no one around to ask for directions and no map or GPS available. How did you feel? Compare that to a time when you were going to a new place and had a map with directions.

_____
_____
_____
_____
_____
_____
_____
_____
_____
_____
_____
_____
_____

EXERCISE 3.1: Help Me Ask the Right Questions

Rationale: This conversation-starter exercise has universal appeal among our patients, families, and providers dealing with different illnesses. People rate these questions as feeling safe, easy to ask, and important to answer at every stage of an illness.

Instructions: Ask your health care providers the following questions throughout your illness. Your family can ask them, too.

Where are we now in the big picture of this illness?

_____

_____

What can we do now to be as well as possible?

_____

_____

What are common signs of this illness worsening?

_____

_____

What are important things to prepare for next?

_____

_____

What organizations and resources can support us?

_____

_____

 Download copies of this worksheet using this QR code.

Exercise 3.2: What Are Some Practical Things to Think About?

Rationale: As your situation changes over time, your needs will change. Planning ahead will keep you feeling organized. This exercise is an example of zooming out on practical things that may get overshadowed by the medical system.

Instructions: Below is a list of topics you will likely need to address at different times during your illness. It is neither comprehensive nor diagnosis-specific. Review the list by yourself or with your family to assess what you have done and what you have questions about. Put a check mark next to items on which you want to follow up. It can be helpful to ask your health care provider to review this list with you and identify which topics you should prioritize now or in the near future.

Daily routines and appointments

Do you need and have support for:
- ☐ Transportation
- ☐ Coordinating and attending medical appointments
- ☐ Managing daily medication
- ☐ Cleaning, laundry, preparing meals, household errands
- ☐ Managing personal finances
- ☐ Personal care (dressing, bathing, toileting, grooming)
- ☐ Exercise, movement, activities
- ☐ Social interaction/companionship

Inner crew, family, and caregivers

Do you need to arrange relief or support for the primary caregiver(s)? If so, which caregiving options are best to consider:
- ☐ Family/friends/community
- ☐ Funded home care supports
- ☐ Privately hired home care
- ☐ Care facility

Living situation

Which living situation best matches your needs for your illness?
- ☐ Current home
- ☐ Current home with adaptations
- ☐ Living with caregiver
- ☐ Assisted living
- ☐ Care facility or nursing home

Personal wishes and family affairs

What needs to be proactively discussed and settled with relevant parties?
- ☐ Critical personal accounts access, passwords, contacts
- ☐ Advance care planning discussions
- ☐ Substitute decision maker/lasting power of attorney for health care designation
- ☐ Will and estate planning
- ☐ Legacy leaving and funeral planning
- ☐ Digital legacy

Support and resources

Which resources should you connect with?
- ☐ Illness-specific and volunteer organizations
- ☐ Rehabilitation programs
- ☐ In-home and institutional care services
- ☐ Social and financial support
- ☐ Psychological support (e.g., bereavement or spiritual counselor, doula, child life specialist, etc.)
- ☐ Peer support and respite/caregiver support

 Download copies of this worksheet using this QR code.

EXERCISE 3.3: Help Me Understand the Big Picture

Rationale: Each illness has a general trajectory. Certain illness-specific signs and symptoms will change over time. The exercise below is meant to help you understand what you will experience as you move from one stage of your illness to the next, so you can anticipate and manage how you'll feel as you shift between stages.

Instructions: Use the form below in conversations with your health care providers to learn about the average symptoms at each stage of your specific illness. Make notes about what stage you are in (the stage that represents you on most days), what to expect (signs, symptoms, and physical changes), and how to maximize your quality of life. Revisit this exercise over time, especially if you notice changes.

Beginning Stage

What to expect	Notes about how to manage at this stage

Middle Stage

What to expect	Notes about how to manage at this stage

Late Stage

What to expect	Notes about how to manage at this stage

End Stage

What to expect	Notes about how to manage at this stage

 Download copies of this worksheet using this QR code.

EXERCISE 3.4: Help Me Prepare for Different Stages

Rationale: While some patients want to learn about changing symptoms along the journey (see exercise 3.3), often people don't know what to do to prepare for various illness stages. We created this exercise to start the conversation.

Instructions: Below is a table organized around the illness stages. Review the important actions at each stage with your health care providers and inner crew. Review the list of things to think about, and consider what you ought to be planning for now. Because this list is generalized, be sure to discuss if and how these apply to your specific illness, and add additional items that are relevant to you and your situation.

Beginning Stage

Key life changes	Notes about how to manage at this stage
Explore ways to slow progression and lessen symptoms.	Taking medications as prescribed Integrating good nutrition, regular physical exercise, and social engagement Making time for medical visits and rehab programs Getting updated on preventative care (e.g., flu shots) Learning self-management strategies to manage exacerbations and symptom flare-ups Other: _____
Designate person(s) for future health care oversight in case you are unable to express consent and needs.	Substitute decision maker/lasting power of attorney for health care Point person(s) for communication and coordination of care Companion for appointments and tracking of medical information Other: _____
Settle personal affairs proactively, while you can express preferences.	Critical account access, passwords, contacts (e.g., banks, life insurance) Will and estate planning Advance care plan discussions End of life wishes (e.g., legacy leaving and funeral planning) Other: _____

Middle Stage

Key life changes	Notes about how to manage at this stage
Assess needs and get support to maintain your daily routines.	Cleaning, groceries, meal preparation, home affairs Medication management Managing personal finances Exercise, social interaction, and companionship Emotional support Transportation Other: _____
Assess ability to provide care at home and consider professional services.	Assistance with feeding, bathing, hygiene care, dressing, toileting Mobility aids and preventing falls (e.g., walker, cane, wheelchair) Other: _____
Assess home environment to ensure safety and maximize energy and independence.	Making home modifications to prevent injury and/or enable mobility (e.g., walker, wheelchair, stair lift) Enhanced home care supports (e.g., public home care, private home care, community supports) Alternative living arrangements (e.g., one-floor living, retirement home, institutional care) Other: _____
Prevent loneliness and isolation.	Continuing social interaction/companionship Other: _____
Identify and support family caregivers.	Finding resources, supports, and strategies to prevent burnout Other: _____

Late and End Stage

Key life changes	Notes about how to manage at this stage
Discuss and make decisions about end of life, with a focus on quality of life.	Returning to advance care planning discussions to inform decision-making
	Do-Not-Resuscitate/Allow Natural Death designation
	The burdens of artificial nutrition and hydration
	Understanding what natural dying looks like for your illness
	Seeking resources for grief and bereavement support
	Other: _____

 Download copies of this worksheet using this QR code.

EXERCISE 3.5: Help Me Draw the Trajectory of My Illness

Rationale: Some people find it helpful to see the trajectory of their illness to date. Visuals can reinforce what the overarching pattern of your illness will look like and can help you communicate to others where you are in your journey.

Instructions: Use the graph below in two ways:

1. Draw your own medical history and the trajectory of your illness from diagnosis to present day, including important dates and significant medical events (e.g., hospitalizations, start of treatments, surgeries, etc.). Share this when meeting with new health care providers.

2. Ask your health care provider to draw a line that shows their understanding of the trajectory of your illness, including how your health or stamina will change over time. You might ask for an average pattern of the illness, and perhaps where they think you currently are on that general pattern. If the provider knows you well, together you might personalize the graph to show how things have changed for you over time, from diagnosis to present day, and what the future line might look like. In either case, you might also ask how long the average timeline is for the average person with your illness.

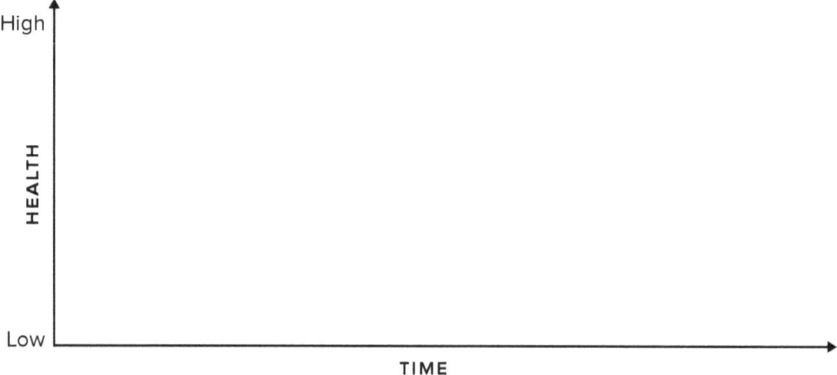

 Download copies of this worksheet using this QR code.

FAQs: Zoom Out

How do I respond when my health care provider is resistant to my questions about the big picture? Often, I'm told "it varies from person to person" or "there's no crystal ball."

Try explaining why you're asking this question. You could say something like, "My understanding is that this illness has a general pattern to it. I'm looking for a general idea about the stages of this illness to better understand where I'm at and what to expect if I need to make plans or decisions later. I know that every patient is different, so I'm not asking you to predict my unique story. Instead, can you tell me what the average person with this illness would experience?"

Where can I get information about the big picture of my illness?

Because we are talking about the general pattern and natural history of your illness, there are multiple sources. These can include Internet searches from reputable websites (e.g., national health or disease-specific organizations, academic hospitals, etc.), which could include AI chatbots or virtual assistants; health care providers (all interprofessional health care providers have some level of information about this, so depending on who has time and rapport with you, you can ask them to speak to the big picture to the extent of their scope of practice or experience); specialist clinicians; your family doctor or primary care team; disease-specific societies (websites or local support groups); and endorsed books and podcasts about your illness.

You can do your research first and go to your appointment to share your understanding of where you are at and where things are going. You can ask the clinicians to confirm if your information is correct or not.

How do I zoom out if I have more than one life-changing illness?

If you have multiple illnesses, you should do the exercises in this chapter for each one. Then talk to your health care providers to understand the overlap between your illnesses.

What if my loved one doesn't want to zoom out, but I do?

Not everyone has the same readiness for information at the same time or moves at the same pace. This has to be respected. However, what can be helpful is reminding the other of why getting this information is important. If they are not ready now, you may want to revisit this again later. (Refer to the chapter "Know Your Style.") This doesn't mean everyone has to wait. You can seek this information for yourself. You can do research on your own time and in your own space and still respect your loved one for wanting less information.

I want to zoom out with my aging parent, who has dementia. For various reasons, I cannot attend all the doctor's appointments. When I call the doctor's office for updates, they won't share information with me, and when I ask my parents, they tell me everything is fine. What am I to do?

Legally, clinicians can share personal health information only with the patient. The exception is when people are found incapable of making their own health care decisions—for example, because of cognitive impairment. However, a patient can consent to give other people access to their health information. So, in this case, ask your parent to give their doctor permission to share medical information with you and to document this permission in the medical chart. Permission can also be given to share information by phone. It's best to clarify the sharing of information early in an illness, especially if cognitive decline is anticipated. Don't forget that you can get started on zooming out about dementia by doing some of your own research.

FOR MY BIG PICTURE

Which statements represent you best? Circle all that apply.

a It is important for me to know the overall pattern of my illness.
b I want to know where I am at in my illness.
c I would like to be able to identify when I am entering the next stage of my illness.
d I want to understand the average life expectancy and general timeline of my illness.
e Other: _____

_____

4

KNOW YOUR STYLE

Y**OU MAY FEEL LIKE** you're at the mercy of your life-changing diagnosis. The key Know Your Style is about claiming some control over your experience, even though you cannot necessarily change the illness itself. This chapter helps you become more aware of your natural tendencies when you face life challenges. Many frustrations during an illness experience arise from typical family and relationship dynamics. When you know your style and that of your inner crew, you can lean into your strengths and reasonably predict how you will walk this illness journey.

Reflection

Everyone has unique styles of emotional, behavioral, coping, and decision-making patterns in their personality. Some are positive and some are negative, depending on the situation. When people are facing an illness, their styles are often amplified. The goal with this key is to understand yourself better so you have a better experience. It is about harnessing the awareness of your personal approach and how you deal with challenges, to gain more control over your illness story.

Prompt: Consider the emotional, behavioral, and coping patterns you fall into when you are facing a major challenge. What patterns are helpful? What patterns aren't so helpful?

EXERCISE 4.1: Map Your Style

Rationale: We are all unique people; there is no correct or ideal style. However, traits, patterns, and tendencies usually become amplified during an illness journey. This exercise will help you predict how you will walk your illness, for better or worse.

Instructions: Below is a list of traits relevant to a life-changing illness. Circle where you feel you fit on the scale from 1 to 4, where the different ends represent opposite ways to exhibit the trait. At the end of the exercise, read the scoring assessment.

Information-Seeking Style

Wait to be told		Super seeker
When a challenge comes up, you prefer to avoid it and hope it goes away on its own.	< 1 2 3 4 >	When a challenge comes up, you want to learn everything you can as soon as possible.

How You Like to Have Tender Conversations

Sugarcoated		Straight up
You don't like to talk about the negatives and prefer to focus on the positives.	< 1 2 3 4 >	You prefer information delivered in a straightforward way. You like to face challenges head on.

Planning Into the Future

Day to day		Super planner
You like to live life in the moment and go with the flow.	< 1 2 3 4 >	You like to plan into the future, typically making detailed timelines and lists.

Level of Assertiveness

Passive		Assertive
You're naturally more reserved, shy, or introverted. You tend to not ask too many questions or challenge health care providers.	< 1 2 3 4 >	You're not afraid to challenge something or ask questions, even if it makes others uncomfortable. Some might describe you as direct or blunt.

Decisiveness

Indecisive
You often arrive at decisions after consulting with everyone and sometimes are accused of "sitting on the fence" and not making decisions. This is typical of "people pleasers."

< 1 2 3 4 >

Decisive
You make decisions clearly and on your own. This is typical of "take charge" people.

Coping Mechanisms

Unhealthy patterns
You have a history of unhealthy coping mechanisms, e.g., avoiding talking with others, isolating yourself, drinking alcohol, stress eating, etc. These sometimes lead to other issues.

< 1 2 3 4 >

Healthy patterns
You have a lot of healthy coping mechanisms, having practiced dealing with stressful situations before, e.g., yoga, walks, exercise, meeting friends.

Need for Privacy

Private
You may be comfortable spending lots of time alone. You prefer to keep health or personal matters to yourself.

< 1 2 3 4 >

Open
You're comfortable sharing personal news with others. You enjoy spending time in large groups and at social functions. You are often gregarious and outgoing.

Organization Style

Disorganized
You have a hard time keeping track of things. You often miss important dates or appointments.

< 1 2 3 4 >

Organized
You have a system to keep track of complex information, such as calendars or notebooks, to record dates and times of appointments.

Another Trait That You Feel Is Important to Describe You

< 1 2 3 4 >

Scoring Assessment

Information-Seeking Style

Wait to be told: The benefit is that avoidance is sometimes a powerful coping and survival mechanism. It allows people to keep going and face each day. Watch out for increasing anxiety, as the challenges of the illness don't typically disappear on their own, and often grow.

Super Seeker: The benefit is that seeking information can keep you feeling grounded, in control, and ready for twists and turns. Watch out for becoming overwhelmed by too much unfiltered information. You may also get frustrated that you are working faster than the system, and may feel annoyed when your questions are not answered.

How You Like to Have Tender Conversations

Sugarcoated: The benefit is that this style may offer you a temporary degree of hope. Watch out for avoiding the reality of your situation. Your hope can get stuck in an unrealistic wish. People around you may feel silenced.

Straight up: The benefit is that you are more likely to adjust to every change in your illness. Your hope will evolve and match the reality of your situation. Watch out for people around you who may not be as open to the reality of the illness as you are. You may get frustrated when health care providers avoid speaking directly.

Planning Into the Future

Day to day: The benefit is that this can help you face the immediate tasks and challenges. It can help you cope in the short term. Watch out for feeling chaotic and unmoored. If you don't plan much, you may feel like you're always playing catch-up and jumping from one crisis to the next.

Super planner: The benefit is that you are more likely to feel more in control. You will be more prepared for the twists and turns of the illness when they happen. Watch out for becoming frustrated by unexpected twists. When things don't go as planned, you may feel unbalanced. It may frustrate you if you feel you don't have the information you need to make plans or when there are periods of uncertainty.

Level of Assertiveness

Passive: The benefit is that this often means appointments go smoothly and efficiently. Watch out for the likelihood that you will be offered standard or generic care instead of individualized care. If you have questions that go unanswered, this could breed anxiety and fear.

Assertive: The benefit is that you are more likely to represent yourself as unique. You will be able to make decisions that suit you best. You will advocate for yourself. Watch out for feeling contrarian. Health care providers may not react as you wish or answer your questions. They may get frustrated when your agenda throws off the flow of the appointment for them.

Decisiveness

Indecisive: The benefit of consulting with others to help you make decisions can provide different perspectives and help those you turn to feel included. Watch out for taking more time than is necessary to move forward and for being swayed by strong opinions that may not match your needs. You want to be aware of defaulting to standard care that does not represent what you want.

Decisive: The benefit is that you will represent your best interests, even if not everyone is happy. You will make decisions quickly. Watch out for feeling frustrated that you are working faster than your inner crew or health care providers. You may need to explain your decision-making process so others are on board.

Coping Mechanisms

Unhealthy Patterns: The benefit is that you may feel temporary relief and a sense of release when you do these behaviors. Coping mechanisms are a way to survive until the next day and feel temporarily less overwhelmed. Watch out for feeling increased fear and anxiety. You may struggle with your inner self and have difficulty adapting and moving forward. You may struggle in your relationships, as there is only temporary relief.

Healthy Patterns: The benefit is that you will continue to take care of yourself and feel a sense of control. You will feel more like yourself. Watch out for frustration when you can't employ your typical coping mechanisms because of time or physical limitations. You will need to adapt these important behaviors as needed.

Need for Privacy

Private: The benefit is that you feel like you are putting less burden on others. You don't want to inconvenience others, or you believe it is not their business. Watch out for isolation, not knowing how or when to ask for help, or difficulties accepting help when it is offered. You may feel invaded and exposed as others start to enter your life to support you.

Open: The benefit is that you will engage others in your journey. They will feel less helpless. You are more likely to accept help and be less overwhelmed. Watch out for other people being uncomfortable with your frankness about your situation.

Organization Style

Disorganized: The benefits are that you likely have time to enjoy the moment, are spontaneous and flexible, and don't get stressed out by minor details. Watch out for a chaotic illness journey and feeling out of control. You are more likely to need someone to walk this journey with you and become your illness manager.

Organized: The benefit is that you will feel in control and not overwhelmed. Watch out for frustration with the health care system, which can be fragmented and siloed. You may get annoyed when others are late or missing information.

EXERCISE 4.2: Mix and Match

Rationale: You can mix and match with your inner crew to balance out your strengths with potential pitfalls. For instance, if you tend to be disorganized, you might identify someone who is organized to keep track of important details. You want to have realistic expectations for yourself and others as you blend your individual styles and strengths.

Instructions: Ask two important people in your inner crew to complete the same traits quiz you completed for yourself in exercise 4.1. If you know your people well, you might complete it on their behalf. To identify ways to be most supportive, inner crew members can do this exercise, even without a patient's involvement.

Name: _____

Information-Seeking Style

Wait to be told
When a challenge comes up, you prefer to avoid it and hope it goes away on its own.

< 1 2 3 4 >

Super seeker
When a challenge comes up, you want to learn everything you can as soon as possible.

How You Like to Have Tender Conversations

Sugarcoated
You don't like to talk about the negatives and prefer to focus on the positives.

< 1 2 3 4 >

Straight up
You prefer information delivered in a straightforward way. You like to face challenges head on.

Planning Into the Future

Day to day
You like to live life in the moment and go with the flow.

< 1 2 3 4 >

Super planner
You like to plan into the future, typically making detailed timelines and lists.

Level of Assertiveness

Passive
You're naturally more reserved, shy, or introverted. You tend to not ask too many questions or challenge health care providers.

< 1 2 3 4 >

Assertive
You're not afraid to challenge something or ask questions, even if it makes others uncomfortable. Some might describe you as direct or blunt.

Decisiveness

Indecisive
You often arrive at decisions after consulting with everyone and sometimes are accused of "sitting on the fence" and not making decisions. This is typical of "people pleasers."

< 1 2 3 4 >

Decisive
You make decisions clearly and on your own. This is typical of "take charge" people.

Coping Mechanisms

Unhealthy patterns
You have a history of unhealthy coping mechanisms, e.g., avoiding talking with others, isolating yourself, drinking alcohol, stress eating, etc. These sometimes lead to other issues.

< 1 2 3 4 >

Healthy patterns
You have a lot of healthy coping mechanisms, having practiced dealing with stressful situations before, e.g., yoga, walks, exercise, meeting friends.

Need for Privacy

Private
You may be comfortable spending lots of time alone. You prefer to keep health or personal matters to yourself.

< 1 2 3 4 >

Open
You're comfortable sharing personal news with others. You enjoy spending time in large groups and at social functions. You are often gregarious and outgoing.

Organization Style

Disorganized
You have a hard time keeping track of things. You often miss important dates or appointments.

< 1 2 3 4 >

Organized
You have a system to keep track of complex information, such as calendars and notebooks, to record dates and times of appointments.

Another Trait That You Feel is Important to Describe You

< 1 2 3 4 >

 Download copies of this worksheet using this QR code.

FAQs: Know Your Style

Given how serious the nature of the disease is, why won't the patient listen to the doctor's advice and change their habits (e.g., quit smoking or eat healthier)?
Habits are not formed overnight. They are typically long-standing. Not only are habits hard to change, but they also often serve a purpose, such as temporarily soothing, calming, and relaxing a person. You might plan for how to deal with the underlying reason for the habit. For example, come up with another way for the person to relax so they don't need to resort to the unhealthy habit. Badgering someone to change won't help. They have to want to change their habits. Pick your battles.

What if my family member does not want to talk about anything? They are not the kind of person who wants information and are not interested in discussing their style.
You can do exercise 4.2 for other people to the best of your ability, based on your knowledge of them. The assessment will help you understand the people closest to you, highlight things to watch out for, and set your expectations of them accordingly. With respect to people not wanting to know their style, you can try to explain why it is helpful to them. At the end of the day, though, if a person is avoiding information, they are essentially showing their style!

What if a patient is an avoider, doesn't ask questions, won't accept help, and won't talk about the future? As a caregiver, what can I do?
If you reflect back, you might realize that this has been their pattern for their whole life. You may take some comfort in the fact that they are living their illness journey on their terms, even if it isn't the way you would do things. There is no one way to journey through an illness. We often tell people that the silver lining is that you realize these traits about your person. Then you can avoid frustration because you expect these deep-rooted traits to continue.

Some people do change, though... when they're ready. Keep inviting them to do so by offering to share or explore information together, once in a while, but respect that they are being true to who they are. In the meantime, make sure you get your own needs met. You count, too.

There are often different caregivers involved—for instance, a spouse and an adult child—who might not be on the same page about the patient's care. This can lead to much tension. What can be done when two caregivers have different opinions?

In these cases, knowing each other's style is so important. The difference of opinion is often less about the best option for the patient and more about the psychology of the people involved. For instance, if a caregiver won't agree to get overnight help, even though their spouse (the patient) can't walk and is at risk of falling out of bed, then try to understand what's behind the refusal. Do they feel like if they get help they'll be seen as a failure? Do they value only medical opinions from doctors? Are they very private and thus reluctant to have anyone witness the situation? Understanding the reasoning behind the thinking can help you find common ground and reframe the options as a way to mutually achieve goals. Even if you don't agree, you can at least understand the motivation.

FOR MY BIG PICTURE

See exercise 4.1, although your answers may have changed.

	Information-Seeking Style	
Wait to be told	< 1 2 3 4 >	Super seeker
	How You Like to Have Tender Conversations	
Sugarcoated	< 1 2 3 4 >	Straight up
	Planning Into the Future	
Day to day	< 1 2 3 4 >	Super planner

5

CUSTOMIZE YOUR ORDER

THE KEY CUSTOMIZE YOUR Order helps you advocate for yourself. The health care system values standardization and efficiency. Without any opposing forces, the system will treat you like the average person, a statistic, instead of as *you*. Representing yourself to the health care system will increase the likelihood of your being treated as a whole person. Articulating what is most important to you is the best insurance for feeling like yourself throughout the entire illness journey. This chapter shows you how to customize your order to guide your decisions and get care that best reflects your values.

Reflection

Health care providers know the illness better than anyone because they have seen it many times. However, you know yourself best. While they may be familiar with the illness, they will not know your preferences. Reflecting on what is important to you is the start of customizing your order—tailoring your care plan to match your goals and inclinations. Once you've reflected on this, go to your next appointment and tell them, "Here's what you need to know about me to provide me with the best care possible… " Or "Here's what matters most to me… "

Prompt: The Patient Dignity Question, created by Dr. Harvey Max Chochinov, distinguished professor of psychiatry at the University of Manitoba, is "What do I need to know about you as a person to give you the best care possible?" What do your health care providers need to know about you to give you the best care possible? What would you tell them matters most to you?

EXERCISE 5.1: Explore What Makes You Unique

Rationale: Let's get to the core of who you are. After all, life is busy when you have a life-changing illness. You will not often get the chance to reflect on the things you hold in high regard. Getting at your core values will help you bring your unique self forward and guide you through your illness.

The questions in this exercise are meant to highlight what is most important to you, the patient. This exercise might also be useful for a family member who is caring for a patient who is reluctant to talk about their illness but might be open to talking about what matters to them.

Instructions: Take some time to reflect and write down your answers to the following questions.

What matters most to you and why?

_____
_____
_____
_____
_____
_____
_____

What brings you joy?

_____
_____
_____
_____
_____
_____
_____

What gives your life meaning?

Thinking about the way you live your life, what would you not want to give up?

What traits define the essence of you?

EXERCISE 5.2: Define Your Priorities

Rationale: People often find it hardest to assert their values when facing a major decision related to their illness, whether that is to continue working, change medication, stop treatment, or something else. Defining your values now will make it easier to bring them forward later.

Instructions: What are your priorities when making decisions about your care? To answer that question, select up to four values that you would like to drive any decision related to your illness. Below are some examples, though you may want to add your own. Circle between one and four of your top priorities. Then rank them in order in the space provided, with number one being the most important. Once completed, share your priorities with your inner crew.

My priorities that guide me through my illness and decisions are:
- To not be a burden
- To ensure my family is okay
- To leave a legacy
- To not suffer too long
- To retain mental acuity/a clear mind
- To be mobile and active
- To be in nature
- To be surrounded by things or pets or people I love
- To have quality of life
- To live longer
- To repair relationships
- To have autonomy and control
- To contribute to my work
- To make things easiest for my family
- To be economical and cost-conscious
- To be creative and express myself
- To retain my dignity
- To remain at home as much as I can
- To be with my family as much as I can
- To have strong relationships
- To have family harmony
- Other: _____

- Other: _____

My top priorities that will guide me through my illness and decisions are:

1. _____
2. _____
3. _____
4. _____

Exercise 5.3: Conversation Starters for a Medical Decision

Rationale: Your essence should be brought forward many times along your illness journey. This includes when meeting a new care team, making a health care decision, making a change in your personal life, making decisions related to your professional life, deciding how you want to spend time, and determining who you want alongside you through your illness. However, it's sometimes difficult to know how to articulate your priorities to the medical system.

Instructions: Below are some statements you might use as preamble as you introduce your core values to those around you. Circle the one you feel most comfortable with, or use the space to write your own.

a   If we need to make a decision on this, there are important things to know about me to guide this decision.

b   As we explore the options, I would like us to keep my priorities in mind and to stay true to them as we go forward.

c   It's important for me to know that you are aware of my priorities.

d   Create your own: _____

_____

_____

EXERCISE 5.4: Scenarios

Rationale: Now that you've identified and prioritized your values, the next step is to practice applying them in different scenarios.

Instructions: Below are some sample scenarios that might help you practice incorporating your core values into medical decision-making. Record your responses in the space provided.

You are seeing a specialist team for the first time to discuss your treatment plan going forward. How do you ensure they see you as a unique person?

_____

_____

_____

_____

You are offered options A, B, or C. The specialist explains the benefits and burdens of the options. What values will you use as your guiding principles to make a decision that represents you?

_____

_____

_____

_____

A new experimental surgery for your illness is available, but there is a 40 percent chance it will leave you with severe cognitive decline. Is it worth pursuing? What values will help you decide?

_____

_____

_____

_____

Exercise 5.5: Choose a Substitute Decision Maker

Rationale: There might come a time when you lack the mental capacity to make decisions on your own and are unable to speak for yourself. If this happens, health care providers will look to the person who is designated to make decisions on your behalf. The term for this person or persons varies by region and country, but some of the more common terms are "substitute decision maker" and "lasting power of attorney for health care."

Identifying the person you would like to be your substitute decision maker is an important exercise. If you don't legally designate someone ahead of time, the role will automatically fall to a default person whose relationship to you depends on the country and region you live in. This person may not be whom you would want to speak on your behalf. So it's worth investigating the laws where you live, too.

Instructions: The list below suggests the traits your substitute decision maker would ideally have. Think about who might be a good substitute decision maker for you. Then use the checklist below to evaluate how they fare against the suggested criteria.

- ☐ The person understands my wishes and values.
- ☐ The person is someone I trust.
- ☐ The person is capable of making decisions under stress.
- ☐ The person is capable of making decisions in my best interests, even if it conflicts with what they would do.
- ☐ The person is willing and available.

Ultimately, who would you like to ask to be your substitute decision maker?

My substitute decision maker is: _____

FAQs: Customize Your Order

How is Customize Your Order similar to or different from Advance Care Planning?
Customizing your order is broader than advance care planning. This key is about bringing the essence of you to all interactions with the health care system so you have an individualized illness experience based on what's most important to you. The goal of advance care planning is to ensure that during your illness, your substitute decision maker knows you well enough to represent you when a decision needs to be made. Advance care planning also includes discussions to prepare for future decision-making. However, there are many other situations in which your values ought to be brought forward and that do not center on decision-making. These can include things like your ability to pay for medicines, how far you travel to get to the doctor's office, your housing situation, family considerations, and anything about the context of your life to be considered in your care plans. In many ways, Customize Your Order is about making sure you know what you want and can voice it clearly for yourself.

Does Customize Your Order work for everyone? What about people from different cultures, languages, ethnicities, or spiritual beliefs?
Customize Your Order is designed to allow the unique aspects of an individual to be brought forward. These unique aspects often include things like culture, ethnicity, gender, and so on. Some people's cultural or spiritual beliefs might be central to their life, and this should be reflected in their health care priorities. Others may feel that their beliefs are just one of their many priorities. People can also belong to more than one community, and among people belonging to the same culture or faith, there will be variations. Customize Your Order is about making sure all care is adapted to what is important to you.

I have a strong relationship with complementary medicine. What if I prefer alternative treatments, or if health care providers push back on these less conventional options?
Don't be shy. Share your preferences with your health care team. Tell them what is important to you. Ask them questions. But don't expect them to have answers about types of treatments they haven't been trained in. You may

want to ask if you might combine different approaches to your care and what that might look like—for example, if there are any drug interactions between prescription medication and a herbal remedy. Ultimately, you will want to understand the potential benefits and risks of any treatment you choose.

If I don't choose my doctor's recommendations, can I still get good care? I'm worried that if I don't accept the plan, they will be angry or disappointed with me and I will get suboptimal care.
You may have to ask your health care team what it would look like if you don't choose what they have to offer. Ask them if they will still have a role in your care and, if you wish, invite them to still walk this journey with you. Let them know how being linked to the formal health care system will make you feel.

What if the patient cannot speak for themselves? How do I customize the order?
Ideally, you will have had conversations in the past about what they value and what is most important to them. If not, sometimes you have to reflect back on situations or conversations in the past that offer you clues. Did they ever share their thoughts on illness before? How have they lived their life? Go through this chapter and try to answer the exercises with this person in mind. Once you complete the exercises to the best of your ability, you can then trust that your intention is in the right place, instead of using your own values to decide for them.

FOR MY BIG PICTURE

See exercise 5.2. Feel free to adjust your answers if your priorities have changed.

My priorities that guide me through my illness and decisions are:

1 _____

2 _____

3 _____

4 _____

6

ANTICIPATE RIPPLE EFFECTS

THIS KEY IS ABOUT identifying who will be most affected by your illness, and who is in your inner crew—the folks who will support you in various roles. The health system often labels these people as caregivers or carers, and it is not accustomed to partnering with them. Caregivers are at high risk of burnout, and their contributions are often overlooked. But 95 percent of care is provided outside the health system, and most falls on the shoulders of carers and their communities. This chapter acknowledges that your illness is a team affair and shows ways to best support your team.

Reflection

When you are facing a life-changing illness, you will need to rely on others for emotional, physical, and practical support. This isn't easy for everyone. Many of us pride ourselves on our independence and the ability to juggle multiple things in life on our own. However, you will likely need others, and they will need to feel helpful in the face of your illness. Often, this dynamic requires new learning, and shifting your mindset from "me" to "we."

Relying on others is one part of recognizing that you are not alone on this illness journey. Others around you—family, friends, neighbors, colleagues—are affected as well. They will also need to rely on others for support.

Prompt: Reflect on a time when you needed support from others. How did this make you feel? On whom did you rely to support you?

_____
_____
_____
_____
_____
_____
_____
_____
_____
_____
_____
_____
_____

EXERCISE 6.1: Map the Ripple Effect

Rationale: Your illness will affect those around you. Like ripples in water, those closest to you, what we call the first ring, will be most impacted. Those in the second and third rings from the center will be affected differently from those in the center, where you are positioned. This exercise to map the ripple effect helps you identify your inner crew as well as the supporting roles of others beyond your chosen family. Doing this up front will help you and your people understand how they fit into your illness journey.

Instructions: To visualize the ripple effect of your illness, list the people who fit into the first, second, and third rings of your illness.

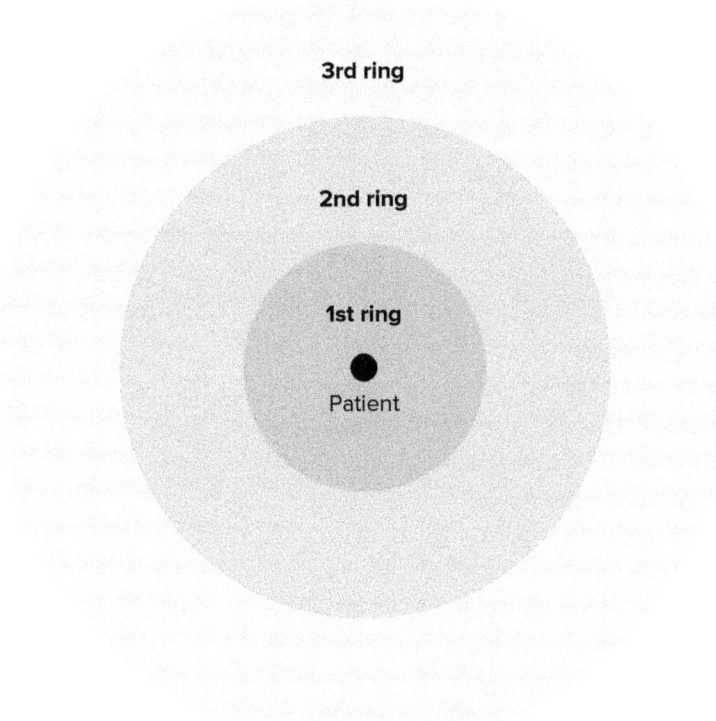

A life-changing diagnosis will impact those around you in a ripple effect.

First ring: This is your inner crew. They are the most emotionally affected by your diagnosis. Typically, this includes your spouse, best friends, your chosen family, children—in other words, those closest to you. People in your first ring are likely going to be involved in emotional, practical, and physical support.

Names: _____

_____

Second ring: Typically, this includes extended family and friends (those you are also close with but who are not your "chosen family"). People in the second ring are likely going to be involved in emotional and practical support.

Names: _____

_____

Third ring: Typically, this includes neighbors, coworkers, and social and community networks (those you might socialize with occasionally). People in your third ring are likely to be involved in practical support, at most.

Names: _____

_____

Tip: All rings are important. Sometimes the most helpful thing that people in the second or third rings can do is support the inner crew rather than the patient.

EXERCISE 6.2: Draft the Job Description

Rationale: From doing the previous exercise, you now have three lists of people affected by your illness in different ways. Next, this exercise will help you identify how people might support you, so you can start to work more cohesively as a team. The goal is to ensure that everyone knows their role and what will be needed of them, recognizing that a person's role may change over time.

Instructions: Reviewing your list of names from exercise 6.1, consider who might support you in the various types of roles below. You will likely put some people's names (those in your inner crew, especially) next to more than one type of support.

Note how often you list the same people under different categories. Whoever shows up the most on your lists is likely going to fill the role of your main caregiver. You may also have more than one caregiver. Name them outright below and do the next few exercises with them.

Types of support	Names
Practical support (e.g., help with errands, banking, groceries, cleaning, housekeeping, transportation)	
Emotional support (e.g., listening to your thoughts and fears, socializing, attending to your feelings)	
Physical support (e.g., help with bathing, dressing, getting up and around, toileting)	
Social support (e.g., help with going to events/getting out of the house)	
Respite support (e.g., giving your inner crew a break if they are tired)	
Spiritual and cultural support (e.g., help with attending to spiritual or religious needs)	

Coordination support (e.g., arranging medical appointments, keeping track of medical information)	
Information seeking (e.g., finding out about available services, etc.)	
Financial/legal affairs (e.g., help with getting wills and legal documents in order)	

My main caregiver(s) is: _____

Tip: A person's role may change over the illness journey, and they may lean in or out more for various reasons. While the patient is the "star," at the center of attention, the inner crew, especially the caregivers, are important supporting actors. You must pay attention to them. Encourage them to share their thoughts, invite them to speak openly, and give them permission to tap out once in a while. Check in on how your people are doing because their emotions and well-being count.

The next few exercises are designed to help you openly discuss your expectations with each other, encourage open dialogue about their role, and prevent burnout.

EXERCISE 6.3: Invite an Open Discussion About Caregiving

Rationale: Sometimes, the caregiver role happens upon a person because they are the only one around, or because you just assume they will take it on. Ideally, the role of the caregiver should be by invitation. It should be discussed and negotiated so the person understands your expectations and feels they have choice.

Instructions: Circle which of the following invitations feels most right for you.

a   I am so grateful you are in this with me. I am aware that my illness has a ripple effect on those around me, such as you. Can we talk about what that is going to potentially look and feel like?

b   I am hoping we will be in this together. Would you be willing to be my caregiver? Maybe we could talk about what that might mean in more detail?

c   You are so important in my life, more now that I have this diagnosis. I will need a caregiver throughout my illness. Can we have a chat about your willingness to do that? What are your expectations? And what do you need to be willing to take on that role?

d   I know everyone assumes you are my primary caregiver, but how do you feel about that? Do you feel ready and able?

e   Create your own: _____
_____
_____

EXERCISE 6.4: Create a Vow

Rationale: You and the people in your inner crew are embarking on an illness journey together. Being in a relationship through an illness journey is challenging in many ways. It's a new type of relationship, almost like a contract or marriage. Stating your commitment to each other is important. We call this "creating your vows" with each other.

Instructions: Create and state vows to each other. Use the example that follows or create your own in the spaces below.

Example

Patient: I, [name], give you permission as my caregiver to take care of yourself. I want you to remain well and need you to know that your emotional and physical health is as important as mine.

Caregiver: I, [name], will be honest with you about how I am doing as your caregiver. I promise to let you know if I am overwhelmed and need a break. I want you to tell me your needs, even if you are worried about overburdening me.

Now you try.

Patient: I, _____

_____

_____

_____

Caregiver: I, _____

_____

_____

_____

EXERCISE 6.5: Create a "Plan B" for Breaks

Rationale: To prevent caregiver burnout, create a "plan B" for when they need a break. Everyone needs a different degree of respite (a break from being a caregiver). Some will do just fine with frequent small sips of respite during the week. Others will need more substantial breaks that we refer to as "gulps." Perhaps these breaks happen less often, but they are just as important. Caregivers may also need longer breaks, a good guzzle, once in a while. For example, the illness course of dementia may span many years. A caregiver will have their own needs over that time. To remain resilient, they are likely to need to sip, gulp, and guzzle.

Instructions: Generate ideas for respite in small sips, gulps, and guzzles. You might also note what you want to have in place so that the caregiver can take a break. This exercise is especially effective if the patient and caregiver complete it together.

Ideas for respite in small sips: _____

_____

_____

_____

Ideas for respite in gulps: _____

_____

_____

_____

Ideas for respite in guzzles: _____

_____

_____

_____

EXERCISE 6.6: Caregiver Self-Reflection

Rationale: This exercise is wholly for caregivers. When caregivers put their own needs aside and soldier through, they tend to get overwhelmed. Then we end up with two or more patients instead of one. We always feel relieved when we meet caregivers who know themselves well, what they can handle, and what they need.

Instructions: Answer the following questions to guide your self-care in the role of caregiver.

What in your life gives you the energy you need to continue?

_____

_____

What are your limits? What are you not comfortable doing?

_____

_____

What are the signs you might be burning out?

_____

_____

How might you declare you need a break? Think of a few ways.

_____

_____

When you take a break from caregiving, who will cover for you?

_____

_____

FAQs: Anticipate Ripple Effects

What should I do if I don't have an inner crew?
Think about who you interact with on a daily, weekly, monthly, and yearly basis. Your inner crew can consist of people who may or may not be related to you. We know one person whose inner crew was their cleaning person, an old colleague, and a distant cousin. This is why it's better to identify your people early. If you don't have family, or if they live far away, start to think about contingency plans and what you can do proactively, such as remote monitoring, hiring help, exploring social assistance programs, and so on. Seek out community organizations that have expertise or may be willing to lend a hand, such as faith groups, hospice volunteers, doulas, groups of other people who live alone, and so on.

How can I get the health care system to recognize my caregiver at appointments?
Use the exercises in this book to introduce your caregiver to your health care team (see exercise 7.2). Renewing your vows with your providers (see exercise 8.4) may help. Let your health care providers know that you and your caregiver are a team, you are in this together, and they play a critical role in your care.

What are ways to maintain control and dignity while leaning on others?
Try shifting your thoughts about receiving care. Consider how good your caregiver feels being helpful in the face of your illness, and for people across all your rings to be able to support you in some way. Think about how your strength and bravery affect others. Think about the lessons you are role-modeling to others who admire you: you are showing others how we can care for one another and how this is a very human experience. You can also create boundaries around who is invited to do what, how long visits should be, etiquette for coming by, and so on. You can control many things and maintain dignity.

I'm worried that I am a burden on my family. What should I do?
Needing your loved ones throughout an illness can feel uncomfortable. This is especially true for people who pride themselves on being independent and the "giver." However, people will likely begin to help out in many ways because it is necessary and they feel it is their honor to support you. Allowing

them in will make them feel useful. Many tell us they are returning support they received and feel grateful for the chance to give back. Often, though not always, the benefits outweigh the burdens. However, it is good to check in with your inner crew and see how they are feeling. Remind them to take breaks. Acknowledge that their health is just as important as yours, and that you feel better when you can see they are taking care of themselves. Talk early in the illness about being honest with each other about how things are going.

The patient or primary caregiver is not willing to accept any help. They are at high risk of burning out. What do I do?

You are likely dealing with someone whose style is to be independent, in control, and proud. They tend to say no when others offer to help. When we meet people like this, we explain that accepting help is protective for both patient and caregivers; someone who refuses help eventually starts to fizzle, needing even more help than they otherwise would have and adding stress to an already stressful situation. Let them know that one of the hardest things to do is try on "yes" and accept help. But often, people around you will feel relieved that you accept help once in a while.

7

CONNECT THE DOTS

WHEN YOU FACE a life-limiting illness, you will have two parallel teams: your inner crew and your formal health care teams. Coordinating between various health care providers and your inner crew is a big challenge. Someone needs to take a leadership role and become an illness manager. Typically, the patient or someone in their inner crew takes this on. This chapter shows you how to connect the dots between all aspects of your care, clarifying who are your health care providers and who is the quarterback of your health care team.

Reflection

Every illness is like a major complex project, with multiple people and many moving parts. Recognizing that you and your inner crew need to make the links between fragmented health care providers is critical to enacting this key.

To avoid feeling overwhelmed, being organized—keeping track of information and appointments—is an important strategy. As well, connecting the dots so that everyone knows what the other people in the team are doing will safeguard against chaos.

Prompt: Think about a time when you completed a complex project involving many different people and multiple moving parts. How did you do it? What would you do differently?

EXERCISE 7.1: Identify Your Illness Manager

Rationale: Patients with someone in their inner crew who is very organized and good at coordinating things—who acts as an "illness manager"—have better illness experiences. You might already have identified this person in the coordination role when you completed exercise 6.2: Draft the job description.

The manager does not necessarily have to be the same person as your caregiver. It depends on the situation, the caregiver's natural tendencies and skills, and the caregiver's health. The patient might also be the manager. You might be the type of person who likes to take charge and is naturally organized and detail-oriented. In this case, choosing a vice manager is wise in case you need backup.

Instructions: Below we list some traits your illness manager ideally has. Think about who might be a good illness manager for you. Then use the checklist below to evaluate how they fare against the suggested criteria.

- ☐ The person communicates well with my inner crew.
- ☐ The person is organized.
- ☐ The person can keep track of many moving parts.
- ☐ The person is someone I trust.
- ☐ The person is capable of making decisions under stress.
- ☐ The person can communicate clearly to health care providers.

After considering the above qualities, who would your illness manager be? Don't forget to make sure to ask if they are willing and available to take on this role.

My illness manager is: _____

My illness vice manager is: _____

EXERCISE 7.2: Identify Your Health Care Providers

Rationale: This exercise will identify the cast of providers who make up your health care team. It will help you understand their roles and who does what.

Instructions: Use the form below to list any and all health care providers who are important to your care and well-being. You can include roles such as your various specialist doctors, family doctor, nurses, social worker, home care workers, physical therapists, occupational therapists, care coordinators, pharmacists, and so on. Write down their contact info and how and when it's appropriate to contact them. State what you understand is their role in your care, and if you aren't sure, ask them. Note that you can add or remove the names of health care providers as things change. After completing this form, share it with your health care providers to confirm that the information is correct, especially about their roles. They might also find it useful to know which other health care providers are involved in your care.

Health care provider name and specialty and/or organization	How to contact them	Their role and what you contact them for
Dr. S, Family doctor, Lakeview practices	office: XXX-XXXX mobile: XXX-XXXX. name@email.com Call if after 5pm or weekends, text or email if any emergency issues	Helps me understand all my results and cares for all my health care needs

 Download copies of this worksheet using this QR code.

EXERCISE 7.3: Identify Your Health Care Quarterback

Rationale: Often, one provider is responsible for your overall care—the one you see often and who has a holistic view of your treatment plan. The health care system usually refers to this role as the "most responsible practitioner." We refer to this person as the "quarterback" of the health care team. As the provider who is primarily responsible for your care, they should be coordinating between different members of your health care team.

Instructions: Having listed your health care providers in the previous exercise (7.2), identify the provider who is the quarterback of your team. If you aren't sure, you can ask them if they see themselves as your most responsible practitioner.

The quarterback of my health care team is: _____

Tip: Do you know who to contact for after-hours help? If not, ask the quarterback of your health care team what to do and who to contact if you have a crisis after hours or on the weekend.

EXERCISE 7.4: Keep Track of Your Medical History

Rationale: Every time you meet a new health care provider, they will want to review your medical history, which has a few crucial elements that are important to keep track of. The illness timeline is a chronological account of the main features of your illness from the time you knew you were unwell. The medical system often refers to this as the "history of presenting illness" or "current illness history." You will be asked other standard questions, such as about other illnesses or surgeries you've had, allergies, and your current medications.

Instructions: Track your medical history below and bring it to your appointments with new health care providers. You may also want to keep a copy in an accessible place, such as in your phone photos or on your fridge.

Current illness history: List events leading up to your diagnosis, how you got your diagnosis, and when. Include major tests, procedures, treatments, and dates of any hospital stays.

_____

_____

_____

_____

Past medical history: Share a list of all the other health care conditions you've had, other specialists you see (e.g., if you are seen for other chronic conditions), and major surgeries (with approximate dates).

_____

_____

_____

_____

Current medications: List the names of medications you take, the dosages, how often you take them, and the date you started them. You may also keep a separate list of medications you were on in the past and when you stopped taking them.

_____

_____

_____

_____

Allergies: List environmental, food, and medication allergies, along with the main symptoms you experience related to these allergies.

_____

_____

_____

_____

 Download copies of this worksheet using this QR code.

FAQs: Connect the Dots

What is the best way to keep track of everything?

This is up to you. Some people like spiral-bound notebooks, others prefer electronic documents or apps. At the bedside, we've seen calendars, whiteboards, chore charts, files, and binders. Virtually, we've seen communication apps, group chats, spreadsheets, shared Google documents, mass email lists, and so on. Whatever works!

Do health care teams talk to each other?

Unfortunately, not all parts of the system are seamless. Multiple institutions may be involved in your care, each with their own records and systems that may not be connected to one another. You may have to act like a carrier pigeon, offering the details of your illness experience across teams, systems, and institutions. The exercises in this chapter will help with that.

When is it most important to connect the dots?

Connect the dots especially during transition points, when chances are higher that important information may fall through the cracks. Transition points happen when your condition is changing and different care locations or new health care providers become involved. Major transition points include:

- right after the diagnosis
- when making decisions about treatment (to start, continue, switch, or stop)
- after any emergency department visit or admission to hospital
- when transferring between care settings
- when you notice you are changing (new or worsening symptoms, change in function or ability)
- when making decisions about work, taking a trip, considering a leave of absence, place of care, or goals of care
- when referred to a new care provider
- when starting with a new service or support program

FOR MY BIG PICTURE

Gather information about the key players on your team into one place. You may want to refer back to exercises 5.5 (substitute decision maker), 6.2 (caregiver), and 7.1 (illness manager).

Caregiver(s): _____ contact: _____

Illness manager(s): _____ contact: _____

Substitute decision maker(s): _____ contact: _____

Other key members of my inner crew:

_____ contact: _____

_____ contact: _____

_____ contact: _____

_____ contact: _____

_____ contact: _____

8
INVITE YOURSELF

SOME PEOPLE WAIT to be invited to share what's on their mind at doctor's appointments. By the time the doctor completes their agenda, the visit is over. Taking a passive approach to your care will place you on the metaphorical conveyor belt of health care: you will feel like a number, your care will be generalized, and you will feel in the dark. This key is about taking charge of your own care, bringing your voice and values forward. You can learn to be respectfully assertive in your illness story so that you remain *you*. Don't wait be invited. Invite yourself!

Reflection

Speaking up during an illness experience may be hard for many reasons. You might be scared no one will listen to you. When there is a power imbalance and you feel intimidated, you may find yourself relinquishing your voice to others. Finding ways to initiate conversations and voice how you feel or what you want, with family members or health care providers, is crucial. It will give you more control of your experience and invite them to follow your lead.

Prompt: Think of a time in your life when you had to advocate for something or someone. What was that like? How did it feel? Did it come naturally?

EXERCISE 8.1: Understand Passive vs Respectfully Assertive vs Aggressive

Rationale: Whether you tend to be passive, assertive, or aggressive by nature will affect the degree to which you are in the know along your illness journey.

Instructions: Check the boxes with the qualities below that best represent you. Which column best reflects your vibe?

Passive	Respectfully Assertive	Aggressive
☐ Saying nothing	☐ Being direct or blunt	☐ Being prone to anger
☐ Keeping feelings to yourself	☐ Being emotionally honest	☐ Holding hostile beliefs
☐ Avoiding confrontation	☐ Sharing opinions	☐ Being physically threatening
☐ Not asserting yourself	☐ Balancing your needs with needs of others	☐ Hurting someone emotionally
☐ Putting the needs of others first	☐ Saying no without feeling guilty	☐ Name calling, mocking, or yelling

Passive. If you tend to be passive, you might constantly feel invisible as a person. Deeper into your illness, you risk looking back with regret that you did not better advocate for yourself.

Respectfully Assertive. Being respectfully assertive can help you express yourself, stand up for your point of view, and earn the respect of others.

Aggressive. If you tend to be more aggressive, you may constantly feel you are at odds with your inner crew and health care team.

Tip: If you are having trouble being respectfully assertive, identify someone in your inner crew who embodies these qualities. Bring them to appointments. Have them advocate on your behalf and ask questions you want answered.

The person who is going to help you be respectfully assertive, advocate for you, and represent your voice (your own name is an option) is:

_____

EXERCISE 8.2: Strategies to Invite Yourself

Rationale: For passive people, becoming more assertive involves developing skills that allow them to express themselves confidently and respectfully.

Instructions: Below is a list of strategies you could employ to be more prepared for interactions with health care providers and that will support you to find your voice. Place a check mark next to ideas you might try.

☐ Prepare for appointments (research your condition the best you can).

☐ Prioritize your questions. Write them down.

☐ At the beginning of the appointment, indicate that you have a few burning questions to ask at some point before the appointment ends.

☐ Bring a support person and take notes or ask permission to tape the session.

☐ Schedule regular appointments, as appropriate, to check in about expected changes in the illness, rather than waiting for an urgent issue before making an appointment.

☐ If you run out of time, make a separate and potentially longer appointment to answer your questions.

☐ Share with the health care provider the names of the crucial members of your informal care team/inner crew.

EXERCISE 8.3: Ask Open-Ended Questions

Rationale: Invite Yourself is about trying to gain as much knowledge as possible. One of the best ways to do that is to ask open-ended questions (rather than closed questions that evoke yes or no answers). An open-ended question starts with "What," "When," "Who," "How," or "Why." The person responding can then offer all their expertise, which might include knowledge you didn't know was available.

Instructions: Before your next appointment, write down all your questions in the space below. Don't edit yourself, just brain dump.

Now reread your questions. Do any need to be converted to open-ended questions?

Examples

Original question (closed question):	Revised question (open-ended question):
Do you have after-hours on-call services?	What would you advise me to do if I have an urgent issue and it's after 5 p.m. on a weekday?
Is walking the best exercise for me, as a patient?	What kinds of exercises are best for me?

Now you try.

Original question	Revised question

EXERCISE 8.4: Renew Your Vows

Rationale: It is helpful to sit down with the quarterback of your health care team (see exercise 7.3) to find out if and how they will be there for you as your illness progresses. We call this Renew Your Vows because it reminds us of when life partners renew their vows after being together for a long time.

Instructions: Ask the quarterback of your health care team (aka the most responsible practitioner) the following questions. Use the space provided to record their answers.

How do you care for your patients across their entire illness trajectory? What happens if your patients start to decline?

_____

_____

_____

_____

How comfortable are you with speaking openly about the long view of the illness? (Declare your preference for how open you would like them to be.)

_____

_____

_____

_____

Who are the other members of your team, such as nurses or coordinators? Who on your team is responsible for what?

_____

_____

_____

_____

Whom do I call if I have an urgent issue or important question?

_____

_____

_____

How does your practice work and communicate with other health care providers, including from other disciplines or organizations?

_____

_____

_____

How do we stay in an efficient communication loop? Whom should I call for what issue? How do I share information if I notice changes in my condition?

_____

_____

_____

What other supports does your team offer—for example, telephone support, after-hours care, and/or home visits?

_____

_____

_____

Tip: This a long list of questions. You might want to organize them by level of priority and ask only one or two at each visit, or set aside a specific visit to ask them all. Don't be disappointed if you cannot get answers to them all at once. The key is to understand if and how the quarterback will journey with you over the long haul.

FAQs: Invite Yourself

Advocating for oneself is difficult. What additional resources are there for people from underrepresented communities to help them invite themselves?

People from underrepresented groups face many additional barriers when advocating for themselves within health care. Experts we've met through our research and podcast recommend that people research, connect with, and get support from trusted organizations that represent and advocate for their community. We advise connecting as early in an illness as possible. Various resources (many free of charge) are aimed at empowering individuals from underrepresented communities and improving their health care experiences. They may include access to health care navigators or social workers, support groups or peer networks, curated reading materials, financial supports, assistance programs, language services, community health workers, interpreter services, and more. These resources can be found in person locally, online, and through national or international organizations. Speaking with members of your community who have faced similar health issues can also be very helpful.

If I am assertive, will I be labeled as a difficult patient and receive bad care?

Being respectfully assertive ensures your needs are met. But some health care providers might perceive assertive patients as difficult. Use polite language and a respectful tone. Be prepared and prioritize the critical issues because time constraints are nearly always an issue. Providers are humans, too, so try to use language that will keep them from becoming defensive. As the saying goes, "You catch more flies with honey than with vinegar." As well, try explaining the meaning behind your questions and actions. If your provider understands where your questions are coming from, they are less likely to find you difficult.

I tried open-ended questions and they did not work. I'm being met with resistance to talking about how things might progress for me. How do I get health care providers to hear and engage with me?

We learned of an effective technique to handle pushback and manage seeming disagreement. It's called the AEA—acknowledge, explain, agree—technique. First you acknowledge what the other person is saying. You can do this by stating, "I hear you," recapping what you heard, and asking questions to clarify if you've understood correctly. After that, you can explain your side and express your concerns or questions. Finally, try to come to some agreement about next steps, which is often easier after hearing each other out. You could return to exercise 2.4 to consider why the health care provider seems to be avoiding your questions, and what you could say in response.

What are the important times to invite myself?
Invite Yourself is about being brave, finding your voice, and trying to level the power imbalance that exists in health care. Part of this means knowing when to *seek* information and when to *offer* important information. We suggest you *seek* information when you have a doubt, concern, or worry; you need clarification; or you notice a change in your condition. *Offer* information when you transition from one health care setting to another, you meet new health care providers and need to share your history, you feel that important information is missing or not being considered, or you notice a change in your condition.

I am getting discouraged. When things seem so busy and I keep meeting resistance, speaking up is hard.
This feeling is completely normal. Doing these exercises is not easy. We offer many strategies and suggestions. Some might work, some might not. Try asking different providers on your team, too. It's a process and it takes time. The key is to persist. It is your life, after all. Nothing is more important.

9

PUTTING IT ALL TOGETHER

CONGRATULATIONS ON WORKING THROUGH the seven keys! Our book, *Hope for the Best, Plan for the Rest*, and the exercises in this workbook were designed to help you reflect on who you are as a person living with a life-changing illness, and on how you will interact with the people who will accompany you on your illness journey. We hope you gained skills to have the best illness experience possible. Now you will take everything you have learned about yourself to create a snapshot of you, so that everyone involved in your care can "get you" at a glance.

Reflection

At the beginning of this workbook, we asked if you felt more in the dark (reactive, unaware, unsure, depersonalized, overwhelmed, frustrated, and scared) or in the know (prepared, informed, confident, individualized, in control, in charge, and hopeful). We hope that you feel less in the dark after having connected to the seven keys.

Prompt: Think of the seven keys and the exercises you've completed. What has been most useful for you in gaining more information? What have you learned? Did anything surprise you?

EXERCISE 9.1: My Big Picture

Rationale: You can summarize everything you have learned from the workbook in "My Big Picture," a one-page summary of you and the seven keys. It is an invitation to the health care system to know you—to appreciate you as a person distinct from other patients.

Instructions: Refer back to the "For My Big Picture" sections at the end of the chapters in this workbook and fill in the following form with your top answers, or new ones if they have changed since you last completed the exercises. Share the form with your health care team at appointments, and with your inner crew, so they know how you want to engage in your illness journey.

My Name: _____

My Illness(es): _____

_____

_____

My understanding is that my illness(es): Circle the answer most true for you

Cannot be cured (chronic):	Yes	No	Not sure
Will likely worsen over time (progressive):	Yes	No	Not sure
Will likely shorten my life expectancy (life-limiting):	Yes	No	Not sure

Key members of my inner crew

Caregiver(s): _____

contact: _____

Illness manager(s): _____

contact: _____

Substitute decision maker(s): _____

contact: _____

Other key members of my inner crew

_____ contact: _____

_____ contact: _____

_____ contact: _____

_____ contact: _____

Walk Two Roads

Which of the following statements best represents you? Circle all that apply.

a It is important for me to have hope.

b I want to get realistic information about my illness.

c I would like people to communicate with me openly.

d I am not ready for more information yet.

e Other: _____

Zoom Out

Which statements represent you best? Circle all that apply.

a It is important for me to know the overall pattern of my illness.

b I want to know where I am at in my illness.

c I would like to be able to identify when I am entering the next stage of my illness.

d I want to understand the average life expectancy and general timeline of my illness.

e Other: _____

Know Your Style

Information-Seeking Style		
Wait to be told	< 1 2 3 4 >	Super seeker
How You Like to Have Tender Conversations		
Sugarcoated	< 1 2 3 4 >	Straight up
Planning Into the Future		
Day to day	< 1 2 3 4 >	Super planner

Customize Your Order

My priorities that will guide me through my illness and decisions are:

1 _____

2 _____

3 _____

4 _____

 Download copies of this worksheet using this QR code.

CONCLUSION

BY NOW, YOU'VE HOPEFULLY gained skills to obtain person-centered care from any health care provider. The seven keys can help you feel a greater sense of control, choice, and hope, even in the face of a life-changing illness. The keys are not steps or independent of each other. In practice, you will embody all seven keys and incorporate them into the way you walk your illness journey.

The keys represent a mindset that puts the human back at the center of care. This mindset is meant to be used from the beginning of an illness through to the end. At first, it might feel unnatural to enact the keys, but with practice you will find that it becomes second nature. It won't be smooth and easy, so be brave and bold. Persist.

If you have a life-limiting illness, you might hear the term "palliative" at some point along your journey. Don't be afraid to explore, or even embrace, services labeled as palliative care. There's so much fear and misunderstanding around the term "palliative care"—even by clinicians. But contrary to popular belief, palliative care simply means care that focuses on the whole person, values quality of life, and acknowledges human mortality. Palliative care services aim to put your needs and quality of life at the center of your experience.

In fact, this workbook has taught you the essence of a palliative care *approach*. A palliative care approach isn't about dying and death. It's about living as well as you can and still being you during a life-changing illness. You can harness the benefits of this approach by embodying the seven keys, right from the time of diagnosis, regardless of where you are in your illness journey.

Ultimately, this *Hope for the Best, Plan for the Rest* workbook is about enabling you to use the seven keys to live your best life. To get more answers and be more prepared. To be more informed and in the know. To have more choice and control. And to have more hope.

ACKNOWLEDGMENTS

WE COULD NOT ADVANCE a social movement and health care revolution on our own, let alone publish a workbook!

First, we want to thank our incredibly understanding and loving families. Hsien wants to thank Katie, Hannah, Miya, Kelvin, Pau Chern, Linda, and Sue. Sammy wants to thank Mitchell, Lauren, Sarah, Marco, Susan, Danielle, and the rest of her slow-walking crew.

We are also so indebted to Maggie Civak and Kayla McMillan, who have supported us in immeasurable ways. Shout-out to the McMaster research team: Shilpa Jyothi Kumar, Daryl Bainbridge, Joanna Vautour, and Bethany Bocchinfuso.

Thank you to everyone who has invited us to speak at events and conferences, town halls and libraries, hospitals and churches. In particular, there have been many people who were vocal supporters and who energized us to keep going with a workbook. They include Christa Haanstra, Sheli O'Connor, Clare Fuller, Dani Ayre, Lora VanBerlo, Erin Gallagher, Ruth Richardson, Theresa Radwell, Penney Gaul, Rosemary Boulton, Bill Harder, Dipti Purbhoo, Kathryn Mannix, Kathy Kortes-Miller, Harvey Chochinov, C. Elizabeth Dougherty, Jay and Gloria Carusi, Elan Graves, Heather Richardson, Hospice Nurse Julie, and Hospice Nurse Penny.

We also want to thank our cheerleaders and ambassadors from across Canada, the United States, the United Kingdom, Australia, and New Zealand. We are grateful to the many people from around the world who have shared their stories of how this work has impacted them. Finally, thank you to the amazing publishing team at Page Two.

ABOUT THE AUTHORS

DR. SAMMY WINEMAKER is a palliative care physician who cares for patients with serious illness and their families in the home. She is an associate professor at McMaster University in the Department of Family Medicine, Division of Palliative Care. She has won numerous awards for her leadership and palliative care education for health care professionals.

DR. HSIEN SEOW is the Canada Research Chair in Palliative Care and Health System Innovation and a professor in the Department of Oncology at McMaster University. He publishes health care research focused on improving the patient and family experience for those facing serious illness. He was inducted as a member of the Royal Society of Canada's College of New Scholars, Artists and Scientists.

WELCOME TO THE REVOLUTION!

This book is part of a larger social movement called the Waiting Room Revolution. Everyone is invited, including you, to join the movement. Join the global community of patients, families, caregivers, and health care providers who are working to put the human back at the center of care.

THE COMPANION TO THE WORKBOOK

Make sure to check out the original book that ignited the social movement: *Hope for the Best, Plan for the Rest: 7 Keys to Navigating a Life-Changing Diagnosis*. Hailed as the essential guide for every patient and family, it details how to use the seven keys to unlock a better illness journey.

Using real-life stories, it vividly describes the impact on the patient and family experience with and without the keys. It also contains simple action steps, tips, family shout-outs, and additional exercises. Ultimately, it shows you how to get the best care and live well throughout the course of your illness.

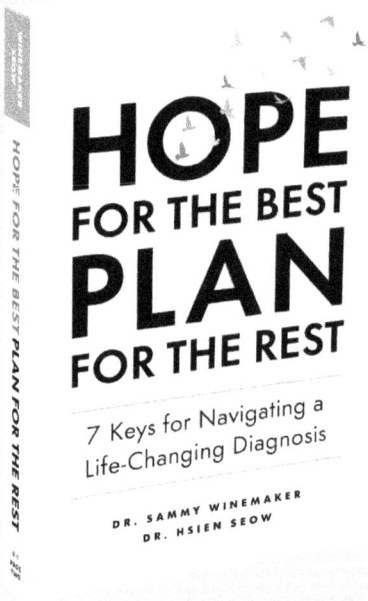

VISIT OUR WEBSITE TO EXPLORE WAYS TO GET INVOLVED!

Learn about our workshops: For patients and families, as well as people wanting to teach this content to others, we created workshop materials that anyone can access.

Join our mailing list: When you sign up, you get access to free resources and information on upcoming events and new ventures.

Listen to our podcast: On *The Waiting Room Revolution* podcast, we interview people from all over the world who share their stories and advice on how to improve the illness experience. Download wherever you get your podcasts.

Become an ambassador: Anyone who believes in this work and is interested in sharing it with others can be an ambassador. Learn more and join the global revolution.

Send us an email if you want information about:
- speaking engagements
- teaching in group settings
- bulk discounts

Connect with us
✉ info@waitingroomrevolution.com
🌐 waitingroomrevolution.com

QR CODE TO FREE DOWNLOADS OF THE WORKSHEETS

Scan the QR code for copies of the worksheets and forms described throughout the workbook. Print, complete, and use them to start new conversations with your family members, caregivers, and, most importantly, your health care providers.

www.ingramcontent.com/pod-product-compliance
Lightning Source LLC
Chambersburg PA
CBHW042358070526
44585CB00029B/2986